The STATE PARKS *of West Virginia*

Stephen J. Shaluta, Jr.

QUARRIER PRESS
Charleston, West Virginia

Quarrier Press
Charleston, WV

10 9 8 7 6 5 4 3 2 1

Printed in China

Library of Congress Number : 2003096898

ISBN : 1-891852-33-7

Book Design:
Colleen Anderson/Mother Wit Writing and Design

Cover photo of Blackwater Falls State Park and title page photo of Shay
Locomotive at Cass State Park by author

Distributed by:
Pictorial Histories Distribution
1125 Central Avenue
Charleston, WV 25302
www.wvbookco.com

Audra

Babcock State Park

Beartown

Beech Fork

Beech Fork

GEORGE WASHINGTON'S
BATH TUB 1748

Berkeley Springs

Blackwater Falls

Blackwater Falls

Blennerhasset Island

Bluestone

Cacapon

Cacapon

Camp Creek

Canaan

Canaan

Carnifex Ferry

Cass Scenic Railroad

Cathedral

Cedar Creek

Chief Logan

Droop Mountain

Droop Mountain

FAIRFAX STONE

THIS MONUMENT, AT THE HEADSPRING
OF THE POTOMAC RIVER, MARKS ONE
OF THE HISTORIC SPOTS OF AMERICA.
ITS NAME IS DERIVED FROM THOMAS,
LORD FAIRFAX, WHO OWNED ALL
THE LAND LYING BETWEEN THE
POTOMAC AND RAPPAHANNOCK
RIVERS. THE FIRST FAIRFAX STONE,
MARKED "FX" WAS SET IN 1746
BY THOMAS LEWIS, A SURVEYOR,
EMPLOYED BY LORD FAIRFAX. THIS
IS THE BASE POINT FOR THE WESTERN
DIVIDING LINE BETWEEN MARYLAND
AND WEST VIRGINIA.

Fairfax Stone

Greenbrier River Trail

Greenbrier River Trail

Hawks Nest

Holly River

Little Beaver

Lost River

Moncove Lake

North Bend Rail Trail

North Bend

Pinnacle Rock

Pipestem

Pipestem

Stonewall Jackson Lake

Tomlinson Run

Tu-Endie-Wei

Twin Falls

Tygart Lake

Watoga

Stephen J. Shaluta, Jr.

In 1985, after nearly 15 years working as a locomotive engineer in my hometown of Grafton, WV, I resigned to become a full time photographer. This is a decision I have never regretted. My primary photography job is as a staff photographer for the West Virginia Division of Tourism, but I also have a successful freelance career.

For more than 20 years I have accumulated a long list of publication credits, through both my Tourism position and my freelance career. These credits include over 300 magazine covers, over 45 calendar covers, and three books. My photographs have also been published in newspapers, magazines, brochures, billboards and books used for editorial and advertising purposes. In recent years the exposure from my website has created an interest for framed and unframed enlarged prints of my photography.

Photography is my passion—my life. Even after 20 years as a professional photographer the joy and excitement is still there. I have recently made the transition and embraced the new and exciting world of digital photography. With more editing control and printing capabilities I can see no limits to my creativity.

I hope you enjoy viewing the photography in this book as much as I have enjoyed shooting it. To see more of my photography and to order prints, please visit my website at www.steveshaluta.com.